◆◆◆ THE ◆◆◆
WONDERFUL
WOODS

ROSE WYLER
PICTURES BY STEVEN JAMES PETRUCCIO

JULIAN Ⓜ MESSNER

Published by Julian
Messner, a division of Silver Burdett
Press, Inc., Simon & Schuster, Inc.
Prentice Hall Bldg., Englewood Cliffs,
NJ 07632.

JULIAN MESSNER and colophon are
trademarks of Simon & Schuster, Inc.

Design by Malle N. Whitaker

Manufactured in the United States of
America.

(Lib. ed.) 10 9 8 7 6 5 4 3 2 1
(Pbk.)   10 9 8 7 6 5 4 3 2 1

Library of Congress Cataloging-in-
Publication Data
    Wyler, Rose.
    The wonderful woods / Rose Wyler ;
pictures by Steven James Petruccio.
    p.   cm.—(An Outdoor science
book)
    Summary: Describes the plants
and animals commonly found in the
forest, including trees, mushrooms,
insects, and squirrels. Suggests
related activities.
    1. Forest fauna—Juvenile literature.
2. Forest flora—Juvenile
literature.   [1. Forest plants.
2. Forest animals.]   I. Petruccio,
Steven, ill.   II. Title.   III. Series:
Outdoor science book.
QL112.W85   1990
574.5′2642—dc20   90-34529
CIP   AC
ISBN 0-671-69166-X (pbk.)
ISBN 0-671-69164-3 (lib. bdg.)

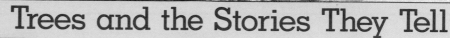

Walk into the woods and
it seems you are walking into fairyland.
No elves sit on the toadstools,
but real live giants are all around you.
The giants make no sound, yet they tell stories
as wondrous as fairy tales.
There are ways you can read these stories
and, as you will see, all are true,
for the giants are trees.

oak

maple

aspen

A woodland tree may have broad leaves
like the oak, maple, and aspen.
Or it may have needles for leaves,
like the pine, spruce, and hemlock.
No matter what kind of tree it is,
its seeds, buds, and wood tell its story.
They tell how it began and how it
grew up to reach the sky.
They tell how it formed a trunk with
branches and twigs and thousands of leaves.

spruce

white pine

hemlock

Tree stories are long for trees live long.
Most of the trees that you find in the woods
are much older than you are.
Many are older than your parents,
and older than your grandparents.
You may even find trees more than 100 years old!

maple seeds

oak flowers

aspen flowers

"Once there was a little seed..."

That's how the story of a tree giant begins.
In trees with needle leaves, seeds form
in cones, between the scales.
In trees with broad leaves, seeds are made
by flowers that bloom in the spring.
Many kinds of tree flowers are small, and so
perhaps you have never noticed them.

Maple flowers make seeds with wings.
Flowers of aspen form fluffy seeds,
while oak flowers form acorns.

Each tree makes hundreds of seeds,
many more than can possibly grow.
Animals eat nearly all of them, yet
here and there a seed is left that stays alive.

Inside each seed there is a tiny plant
with folded leaves and food to give it a start.
To see this plant, soak a seed overnight,
then peel it and split it open.

Outdoors, a seed opens when winter ends.
A root goes down into the ground,
a stem goes up, and leaves unfold.
Later, as the stem grows, twigs and leaves form.

In spring, if you are allowed to, dig up a small tree from the woods. To take it home, wrap its roots and some soil in a bag. Then plant the tree in a flower pot. Water it weekly and it will grow.

The little young tree now has a power
greater than any fairy tale magic.
It can make food from just air and water!
Its roots take water from the soil, then the
water goes up tubes in a layer under the bark.
Veins carry the water into the leaves and there
it is mixed with gas from the air to make food.

◆ ◆ ◆ ◆

Try this. Add some red
food coloring to a jar of
water. Set a twig in it
overnight. Tubes in the
twig and leaf veins will
turn red. Ask a grownup
to split the twig and then
you can see the path
taken by the water.

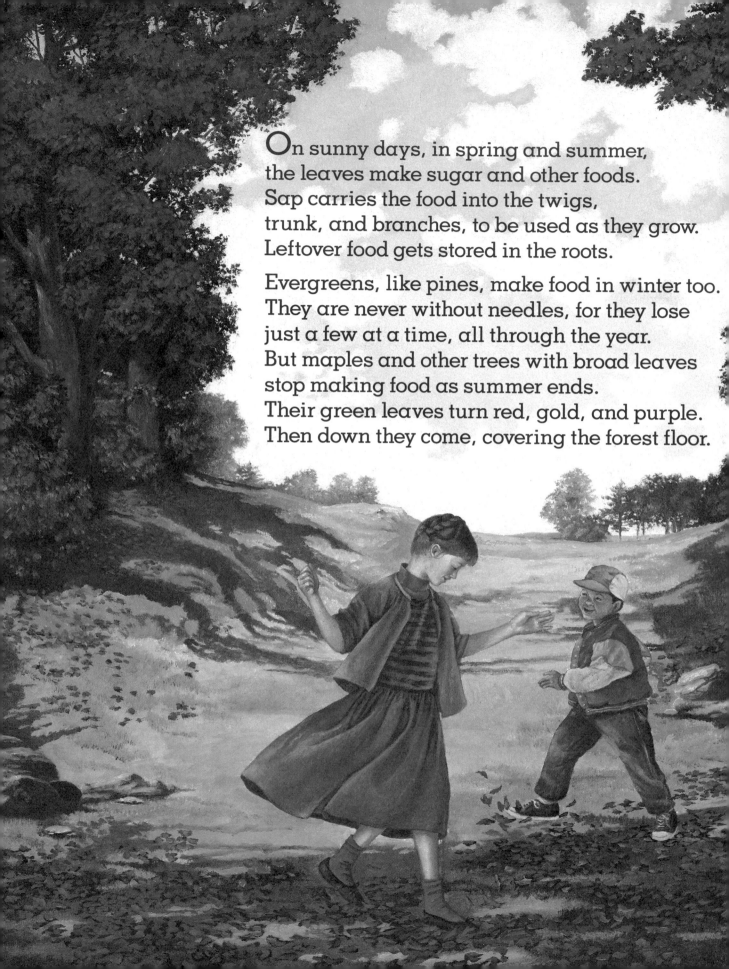

On sunny days, in spring and summer,
the leaves make sugar and other foods.
Sap carries the food into the twigs,
trunk, and branches, to be used as they grow.
Leftover food gets stored in the roots.

Evergreens, like pines, make food in winter too.
They are never without needles, for they lose
just a few at a time, all through the year.
But maples and other trees with broad leaves
stop making food as summer ends.
Their green leaves turn red, gold, and purple.
Then down they come, covering the forest floor.

tip bud

side bud

leaf scar

Why do leaves fall?
Twigs tell this part of a tree's story.
On every bare twig you can see scars that
formed where leaves were joined to it.
The dots on the scars are plugged-up ends
of tubes that brought water to the leaves.
Without water, the leaves dried up and died.
Then autumn winds blew them away.

Even when a tree is bare, it still has leaves—
tiny ones that live through the winter in buds.
Open some buds and you will see these leaves.

In spring, sap from a tree's roots rises
and flows into the buds, bringing them food.
The buds swell until they burst.

On some trees leaves and flowers open from
separate buds; on others, both are in one bud.

Buds on evergreens open too,
and the year's growth begins.

To make tree buds open
in late winter, ask a
grownup to cut off some
twigs. Keep them in a
jar of water in a sunny
place. Change the water
every few days until
leaves and flowers push
out from the buds.

tip bud

side bud

leaf scar

ring

scale scars

one year's growth

A twig grows longer when the big,
fat bud at its tip opens up.
As scales drop off the bud, they leave
a ring on the twig.
This happens every year, so the number
of rings often tells a twig's age.
Can you find a twig as old as you?

Notice the distance between the rings too.
The distance is short in years of bad weather,
but it is long in years that were good
for the tree's growth.

Twigs, branches, and the trunk become wider
as new wood forms underneath the bark.
A band of light-colored wood is made in spring
and summer, and a dark ring is made in fall.
In good years, the bands are wide;
in bad years, they are narrow.

By counting the rings on a stump, you can tell
how old the tree was when it was cut.
If the stump is big, mark every fifth ring.
Then start at the center and you can trace
a tree's life story all the way
from little seedling to forest giant.

Animal Hide-and-Seek

What animals do you see in the woods?
What animals do you hear?
Animals are in the tops and trunks of trees,
on the ground and in the ground.
Some of them stay in dens most of the day.
Some are dull in color and hard to see.
Others hide under logs and leaves.
Forest animals are shy, but you can find them
if you stop along the trail and look and listen.

Chickadee-dee-dee—the bird is calling
its name, chickadee.
The jay calls its name too.
Tap, tap, tap—a woodpecker is pecking holes
in a tree trunk, looking for insects.
Another bird, the brown creeper, creeps
around the trunk while a nuthatch runs down it.
Even when snow is on the ground, these birds
can find food.

Many other birds fly to warm places for the
winter and come back in spring when the woods
are green again and there is more to eat.

woodpecker

chickadee

blue jay

brown creeper

nuthatch

For close-up views of woodland birds,
make some feeders to hang on trees and shrubs.
Supply them with bits of fat, peanut butter,
and seeds, such as sunflower seeds,
and birds will come to eat every day.

But remember to keep the feeders full.
If you hold out some seeds on a jar lid,
maybe a wild bird will fly right up to you.
Stand still and it will eat out of your hand!

17

If a chipmunk comes for your bird food,
watch it pack seeds into its cheek pouches.
The pouches swell up until they are full.
Then the chipmunk scurries off
to store the seeds in its den.
Usually the den is hidden under a tree root.

Leaping around in the trees,
the red squirrel calls, "chickaree."
The gray squirrel makes a different sound,
something like "churrr."
It too leaps from tree to tree.

The big shaggy nests you see high in trees
probably are squirrels' nests.
Both red and gray squirrels build them
and raise young in them in early spring.

For birds, nesting time is late spring.
By then trees are covered with leaves that
hide small nests and baby birds in them.
Whirr . . . whirr—a big bird, the grouse,
takes off from the ground.
Unless a grouse moves as she sits on her nest,
you can walk by her and not see her.
Her coloring blends with the forest floor
and hides her.

If you want to see a bright-colored animal,
look under a log or pile of leaves for a red eft.
Efts are salamanders—relatives of frogs.
They start life in water as tadpoles,
then they grow legs.
After a few years on land, they turn brown
and go back to the water.

◆ ◆ ◆ ◆

**You can keep a red eft in
a jar with moist soil,
moss and ferns. Feed it
once a week with a bit of
chopped meat dangling
from a thread.**

As you turn over stones and leaves, probably
you will find some little gray pill bugs.
This animal is also called a roly-poly bug
because it rolls up in a ball when disturbed.
Count its legs and you find that it has seven pairs.
But an insect has only three pairs, so you know
it is not an insect.
Scientists call it an isopod.
Pill bugs feed on bits of dead matter,
like leaves.
Keep some of them in a jar with moist soil and
dead leaves for a week and see how much they eat.

If you find a centipede, or hundred-legger, don't pick it up with your hands—it bites. A centipede feeds on soft insects and worms. Only a few kinds have a hundred or more legs; the usual number is between thirty and sixty. The millipede, or thousand-legger, has more legs, but not a thousand. Like the isopod, it feeds on dead matter and helps clear the ground for new living things.

millipede

centipede

isopod

The Forest Floor

Every year millions and millions of leaves
fall and litter the forest floor.
Over 250,000 may come from a single oak.
Though a pine keeps its needles two to four
years, it sheds thousands of them yearly.
Yet this leafy litter does not pile up.
Some of it is eaten by animals, but
most of it is destroyed by molds.

Turn over leaves lying on the ground and you see
fuzzy white patches of leaf mold on them.
The mold makes the leaves rot and turn into soil.

Mushrooms, including the ones called toadstools, also help clear the forest floor.
Long threads at the bottom of a mushroom change dead matter into food it can use.
In warm weather, tiny spores fall from its cap and new plants grow from some of them.

The shelf fungus starts from spores too. The shelves grow slowly, as their threads spread in dead wood and destroy it, bit by bit.

Leaves take two to three years to turn into soil
and wood takes even longer.
So there is always some litter in the woods.
In winter, the litter protects roots and seeds
in the ground, and during spring rains
it keeps the soil from washing away.
In springtime, new leaves poke their way up
through the dead litter.
First come the smelly leaves of skunk cabbage
Jack-in-the-pulpit comes next, along with
both white and red trilliums.

jack-in-the-pulpit

skunk cabbage

trillium

While trees are still bare, pale spring beauties
and adder's-tongue dot the ground, and
here and there you find violets—
purple, yellow, and white ones.
Later on, maybe you will find columbine
and pink orchids called moccasin flowers.

Woodland flowers do not grow in great numbers,
and should not be picked.
Anyway, they wilt quickly.

violet

spring beauties

columbine

adder's-tongue

moccasin flower

Ferns follow the early spring flowers.
At first they are fiddleheads with leaves rolled
in a ball that looks like the end of a violin.
The ball uncoils, then lacy leaves spread out.

By late summer, many kinds of ferns look sick.
Brown spots dot the underside of their leaves,
but the spots are not caused by disease.
They are cases filled with spores
that will start new ferns.

Mosses come from spores too.
In the commonest moss, the hairy cap,
the cap is a spore case.
Feathery fern moss is also common.
So is the light green cushion moss.
Since mosses have no roots, they take in
water through their leaves.
They grow in clumps, making a soft rug
for the forest floor.

rock polypody

fern moss

fiddlehead

cushion moss

Even when the ground is covered with snow, mosses stay green.
Plant some in a jar with soil, keep them moist, and they will stay green all winter.
Two kinds of fern remain green too—
the rock polypody and the Christmas fern.
Both grow well indoors.
In fact, the Christmas fern is a popular house plant often sold in stores.

◆ ◆ ◆ ◆

If it is allowed, take a Christmas fern from the woods. Dig up its roots and underground stem. Then plant the fern in a flower pot with rich soil and water it every week.

Christmas fern

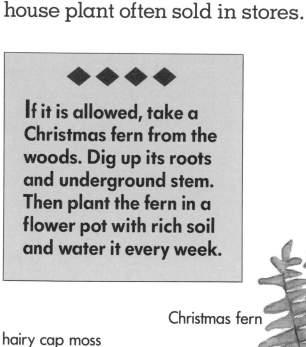

hairy cap moss

fern moss

pin cushion moss

An aquarium tank makes a good home
for plants and small animals from the woods.
First put some gravel on the bottom.
Then add about an inch of clean sand.
Cover the sand with forest soil
and set the plants in it.

Polypody ferns, evergreen seedlings, and mosses
will grow well if molding dead leaves
are spread over the soil.
The leaves will provide food for pill bugs
and millipedes, and the small insects on them
will be eaten by centipedes and red efts.

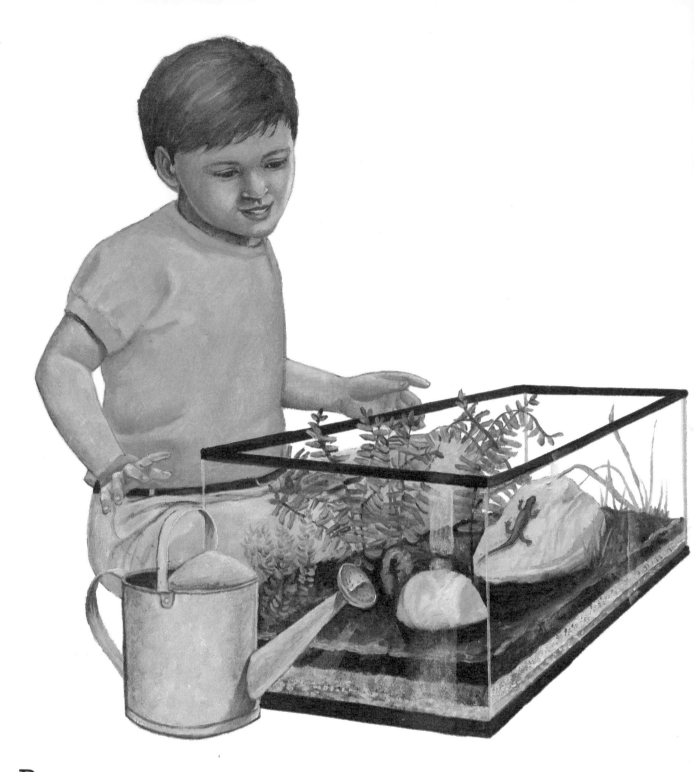

Be sure to keep your indoor garden moist.
Then the plants and animals in it
will live as they do outdoors
in the wonderful woods.